Guided Self-Healing and Mindfulness Meditation:

Multiple Meditation Scripts such as Chakra Healing, Breathing Meditation, Body Scan Meditation, Vipassana, and Self-Hypnosis for a Better Life!

By Healing Meditation Academy

Table of Contents

Guided Self-Healing and Mindfulness Meditation:
Table of Contents
Breathing Meditation

    Easy Breathing Meditation to Improve Mindfulness
    Diaphragm Meditation for Panic Disorders
    Relaxing the Body
    Targeted Muscle Group Relaxation Script
    Relaxation and Physical Hypnosis Meditation

Opening Awareness

    Breathing Awareness and Control Meditation
    Stress and Workplace Awareness Meditation

Abdominal Breathing

    Abdominal Breathing for Oxygenation
    Abdominal Breathing for Impulse Control

Loving and Kindness Meditation

    Kindness Meditation for Self-Care
    Love Meditation for Actualization

Self-Compassion "Break" Meditation

    Forgiveness Guided Self-Healing

Universal Compassion Meditation

    Vipassana Meditation

Anxiety Meditation

    General Self-Healing Script for On-The-Spot Anxiety Relief
    Guided Anxiety Meditation for Active Brains

Introduction

Think about the last time you left work, came home, and actually felt relaxed — not a half-relaxation filled with anxiety and thoughts about the next day – an actual, peaceful calm. For most of us, we might remember this sense of peace last in grade school, or perhaps further back. The pace of our modern world is incredibly fast, and most of us barely had time to notice that suddenly, all of our free time was occupied. Even when we aren't at work nine to five or studying at school – our brains are always working. Thinking. Constant stimuli can be great when it comes to keeping up with your loved ones, but the negative effects of the internet and social media particularly affect our day-to-day mindfulness. You can think of the definition of mindfulness as simply paying attention. Mindfulness places particular importance on focusing the mind, honing your concentration, and really emotionally connecting with what you're centered upon. Mindfulness can center upon anything you choose – if you're stressed about work, thinking clearly and directly about one specific problem can help you overcome it. Meditation comes into play with mindfulness at this stage of thinking clearly and directly. Most of us have, at any given time, more than a handful of things on our minds. Meditating allows you to use your concentration for whittling that handful down. Once you learn how to meditate to quiet your thoughts in order to focus directly on a mindful pursuit, you won't believe the changes you'll experience. Meditation for mindfulness has proven to help individuals be more productive, live their lives with a more positive outlook, and think in healthier thought patterns. Whether you experience anxiety, stress, depression, or simply fatigue from your day-to-day life, taking a moment to compose your thoughts and sink into a deep concentration will abate your symptoms. Many doctors and psychiatrists prescribe meditation with a mindfulness focus as a means of controlling or dealing with difficult life stressors. In order to determine the type of meditation that's right for you, this helpful guide will walk through all the most popular, and effective, style of meditation. Complete with full scripts that will help you center yourself, calm your negative emotions, and bring you peace, each of the following chapters contains everything you need to know about self-healing with guided mindfulness meditations. If you're ready to get started breathing, centering, and freeing your mind, let's dive into the meditation methods that are going to change your life.

Breathing Meditation

Easy Breathing Meditation to Improve Mindfulness

Come into your breath, and your breath will ground you.

Learning to ground your spirit keeps your being whole.

Approach your meditation with an open chest –

Here is air, and there is life.

Allow yourself to settle into a comfortable position, palms open, body relaxed, and stable.

You are in control – it is time to discover the power of your breath.

As you sit, quiet, still, listen to your heart.

Hear the drum – slow, steady. You are a cycle, a pattern, a song.

Inhale for four counts – one, two, three, four,

And exhale for four counts – one, two, three, four.

Your breath brings your life.

Focus all of your mindful attention on the give and take of breathing.

Inhale for one, two, three, four,

And exhale for one, two, three, and four.

Inhale for one, two, three, four,

And exhale for one, two, three, and four.

As you inhale, imagine the universe swelling inside you –

All consuming, you breathe in – and become one.

Inhale for one, two, three, and four –

And exhale for one, two, three, and four – breathe out thanks.

Breathe out appreciation.

Your body, mind, and spirit come alive only with your breath –

And the universe is here to provide for you.

Inhale for one, two, three, four,
And exhale, complete, for one, two, three, four.
Once more, listen to the beating of your heart –
Take three more breaths, focusing on a silent mind and peaceful body.
Inhale for one, two, three, four,
And exhale, for one, two, three, four.
Inhale for one, two, three, four,
And exhale, for one, two, three, four.
Inhale for one, two, three, and four.
True breath brings true peace.
You have centered your breath. Inhale, and exhale, one final time.
Slowly open your eyes. Allow your breath to remain steady.
Go forward.

Diaphragm Meditation for Panic Disorders

You are in control.
There is nothing that can take away your power.
Focus your mind upon only your chest.
Inhale for one, two, three, four,
And exhale for one, two, three, and four.
You are in control.
You are in control.
Call out to your mindful brain –
It is always there, even when you feel overwhelmed.
Call out – focus on finding your mindfulness.
Allow your spirit to quiet.
Inhale for one, two, three, four,
And exhale, for one, two, three, four.
Panic has no place here.
Fear has no place here.
Feel only your breath.

Let your inhales and exhales slow your heart rate.

Breathe in for one, two, three, four,

And expel your anxiety in exhalation – one, two, three, four.

Breathe in for one, two, three, four,

And expel your fear in exhalation – one, two, three, four.

Breathe in for one, two, three, four,

And expel your insecurity in exhalation – one, two, three, four.

Each breath brings life into your being,

Each exhalation takes the pain from your spirit.

Feel your heart rate slowing.

You are calm and in control.

Inhale for one, two, three, four,

And exhale for one, two, three, and four.

As you begin to calm, focus on your lower stomach.

Feel the motion of your diaphragm as you inhale –

One, two, three, four,

And exhale – one, two, three, and four.
Your breath, heart, and belly are your spirit, mind, and body.
Feel your unified being come to peace.
There is no need for fear.
There is no need for anxiety.
Feel your breath.
Inhale – one, two, three, four,
Exhale – one, two, three, four.
Inhale – one, two, three, four,
Exhale – one, two, three, four.
Give yourself permission to find peace.
You do not need to worry.
You do not need to panic.
All is right when your being is centered.
Feel your mindful brain relax,
Inhale for one, two, three, four,
And exhale for one, two, three, and four.
You are light and peaceful – you are safe.
Breathe in for three deep breaths,
And cultivate a safe space for your most anxious moments.
Inhale for one, two, three, four,

And exhale for one, two, three, and four.

With each breath, you solidify the safety of your space.

You are here and protected – in your own existence.

Inhale for one, two, three, four,
And exhale, for one, two, three, four.
Inhale for one, two, three, four,
And exhale, for one, two, three, four.

As you calm and gently move towards surfacing consciousness,

Remember this space you have created.

Hold your peaceful safety sacred –

This cultivated sanctuary is yours.

Any time you feel overwhelmed, return to it.

Return to your mind.

Return to your breath.

Return to your center.

Open your eyes, and go forth with strength

And peace.

Relaxing the Body

When it comes to practicing bodily guided self-healing meditations, the basic outline you'll want to follow is one of focusing, tensing, and relaxing. When you do a bodily relaxation meditation for self-healing, you'll be taking stock of every muscle, system, and reaction. Our bodies can sometimes suffer daily damage that we aren't even aware of. Most individuals hold tension in their jaws, teeth, hands, and shoulders. When you do a bodily relaxation meditation, you will silently take stock of each of your body's aches and pains – in an attempt to relax and bring yourself peace where you need it most. Let's start with a very simple, slow meditation that you can do when you get into bed each night before you go to sleep. Bodily meditations have the added bonus of relaxing your physical being, as well as your emotional side so that you are much more likely to drift into a deep sleep. Once you're ready for bed, lay down on your back with your arms by your side, palms facing downwards on your mattress, legs slightly parted. You can feel free to adjust your position to what's most comfortable for you. However, you should focus on being prone and in a position you routinely like to rest in. On your back is the best possible way to lay with an open chest, an open heart, and an aligned physical being before you begin your meditation – but not everyone's physical body is the same. Find your comfort, and we'll begin. With your eyes closed, walk yourself through the following meditation either once or twice, depending on your body's overall stress and tension.

Targeted Muscle Group Relaxation Script

As your day comes to a close, open your heart and mind to full relaxation.

Gently close your eyes. Feel the dark settle around you like a blanket.

Breathe in through your nose, for one, two, three, four –

And breathe out through your mouth, for one, two, three, four.

Let each exhalation countdown expel negative energy with your breath.

Feel the blood running through your body as you breathe in,

One, two, three, four;

And let your stress and tension dissipate as you breathe out -

One, two, three, four.

You are here, present, and ready for rest.

Let your brain quiet. Focus only on your breath.

Feel your muscles relax as your body fills with oxygen.

Think down to your toes.

What did you do on your feet today?

Are they sore or tired? Focus on your feet.

As you exhale, prepare to tighten your toes as you breathe in.

Inhale one, two, three, four, and squeeze your toes at tight as you can.

Slowly release, exhale one, two, three, four.

Feel the tension in your toes come undone.

Breathe in, one, two, three, four, and shift your focus to your calves.

Exhale one, two, three, four, and tighten your calves as you begin to inhale.

One, two, three, four, tighter, tighter –

And release, for one, two, three, four.

As you move upwards through your muscles, concentrate only on the weight of your own body.

Here, you are present with your spirit, mind, and being.

Each clench and release helps free you from stress.

It is safe to let go. You are allowed to relax.

Think about your knees. Are they tight, or sore?

As you inhale, tighten your knees for one, two, three, and four –

And slowly release, for one, two, three, four.

As you release your knees, press your palms down and feel the ground.

You are here, and your knees, although meant for walking,

Are here to rest.

Think about your thighs. Breathe in and tense, one, two, three, and four –

And slowly release, one, two, three, and four.

Half the tension in your body has dissolved.

You are halfway to a peaceful sleep.

Refocus your mind if your thoughts wander, and think about your glutes.

Did you sit today? Are you tense?

Breathe in and squeeze for one, two, three, and four –

And release for one, two, three, and four.

Your abdomen is the heart of your center.

Slow your muscles slow your breath and pause.

Listen to the sound of your heartbeat.

Your body keeps your heart and spirit safe.

Rejuvenation is key.

Think about your lower back.

Tight, tense, sore.

Breathe in and tighten for one, two, three, four,

And release for one, two, three, and four.

Shift your focus from back to front.

Think about your abdominal muscles.

Think about your stomach.

On an inhale, tighten one, two, three, four,

Squeezing your abs at the top of the inhale.

Release slowly and exhale out, one, two, three, and four.

You are almost done. Feel your muscles nearing sleep.

Moving upwards, focus on your shoulders.

Let them relax, allow them to heal.

Tense and hold for one, two, three, four,

And exhale your release, one, two, three, and four.

Focus once more on the tightness in your shoulders.

This time, press them back into your mattress –

Open your heart and center to full surrender.

Breathe in for one, two, three, and four –

And out for one, two, three, and four.

Come slowly back to rest in a gentle prone position.

Follow your bloodstream down, down –
Towards the tips of your fingers at the tips of your arms.
They are tense like your toes and ready to rest.
Clench your fists as you inhale for one, two, three,
And slowly release your grasp, exhaling one, two, three, and four.
Up from your fingers, focus on your forearms.
Breathe in and squeeze your forearms for one, two, three, four,
And release for one, two, three, and four.
Next, move towards your biceps, up, up.
Flex and clench for one, two, three, and four -
And release – for one, two, three, four.
As we move toward your neck, feel the rest of your body lighten like air.
You are weightless. You are floating.
There is no physical attachment.
You are relaxed, and you are whole.

Breathe in and tense your shoulders up around your neck –

One, two, three, four.

And down, for one, two, three, four.

Shift your focus to your facial muscles. Here, tension is thick.

Through your jaw and mouth, we tend to hold stress.

Feel the muscles in your face, feel your breath entering and exiting your body.

Exist here for a moment, without any motion but breath.

Inhale, one, two, three, four – and exhale one, two, three, four.

Bring yourself down to your center.

Feel your spirit settle.

On your inhale, tighten your facial muscles for one, two, three, and four–

And release for one, two, three, and four.

Once more, return to your bloodstream. You are tired –

Your muscles have calmed,

Your soreness is gone,

There is no more tension.

You are light as air.

As you inhale, think of your body as one complete space.

A unit. A machine.

Your temple.

Exhale one, two, three, and four – and relax.

Sleep comes heavy.

Inhale one, two, three, four, and think about your entire being.

Exhale for one, two, three, and four and feel your breath leave your body.

Your toes, your abdomen, your neck, arms, and legs –

All are at peace.

Inhale, one, two, three, four – and tighten your entire body.

Hold for one, two, three, and exhale –

One, two, three, four.

Let your spirit sleep.

Let your mind rest.

Your physical body is purified.

Think of your palms as you drift off to sleep, pressed against your grounding force.

You are centered. All is quiet.

Allow yourself to sleep.

Relaxation and Physical Hypnosis Meditation

Give yourself permission to engage in self-care.

Find a position in which you are relaxed, comfortable, and open to the universe.

Wherever you find yourself, keep your palms open –

You are receptive to positive energy.

Relaxation of the body and mind rejuvenates the soul.

You are deserving of quiet, and you are deserving of peace.

Now is the time to relax.

Allow your eyelids to droop as you relax your jaw.
Seek out your breath, in through your nose, and out through your mouth.
Hear only the rush of your lifeline breath –

Inhale for one, two, three, and four;
And exhale for one, two, three, and four.
Let the pattern of your breath slow your heart rate.
Feel your toes, legs, and arms fill with air –

Oxygen will help you heal.
Open your heart to a mindful center;
Relaxation only comes once the tension has left.
Imagine, in your mind,
You are a vessel filled with water.
When you begin each day,
You are clear and clean – soft, smooth, still.
The surface is broken, your depths are pure.

There is nothing but love and calm.
As the day goes on,
Your peaceful vessel begins to bubble,
Slowly at first –
A bubble of anger, a rush of anxiety,
A pop of stress.
Your vessel stirs; you are no longer peaceful.
Throughout your day, more and more impurities
Bubble inside you.
Pressure, building, building, building.
Focus your mind on the top of your head.
At the end of the day, you are tight and ready to burst.
There is nothing peaceful about this pressure.
Inhale for four counts – one, two, three, four,
And exhale for four counts– one, two, three, four.
As you exhale, release your vessel's lid –
Allow the pressure to escape.

From your chin to your scalp, release your impurities like carbonated bubbles –

Inhale for one, two, three, four,

And exhale your pressure – one, two, three, four.

Focus on your abdomen, filled with bubbles – tight with pressure.

Release it, up, up, through your scalp, through your mind, out of your being forever.

Inhale for one, two, three, four,

And exhale tension – one, two, three, four.

You are a teapot giving off steam.

From the tips of your fingers up through your arms,

Release the pressure –

Inhale for one, two, three, four,

And exhale for one, two, three, and four.

From the lengths of your legs and up through your torso,

Release the pressure –

Inhale for one, two, three, four,

And exhale, for one, two, three, four.
From the tips of your toes to the top of your head –
Release the pressure.
Purify yourself.
Inhale for one, two, three, four,
And exhale for one, two, three, and four.
Allow your mindful brain to rest; your body is at peace.
All the difficult emotions bubbled up inside you have gone.
You are calm, serene.
You are filled with beautiful water – cool, peaceful, and clean.
There is nothing negative to weigh you down anymore,
You are light and airy,
Soft and clean.
Allow yourself to feel restful.
Allow yourself to feel at home.
Slowly, bring yourself back to consciousness.
You have purified and cleansed.

You are whole again.

Opening Awareness

Plenty of us are too bogged down in our personal lives, work lives, and social lives to realize that we have closed off our senses to awareness. Awareness in mindfulness and meditation often coincides with individuals who wish to control depression or anxiety. While awareness meditations aren't a total cure for these types of emotional disorders, opening your heart and mind to being aware of yourself, your surroundings, and your day to day life can have a huge impact on your happiness. Oftentimes referred to as a "frame shift," awareness will bond

Breathing Awareness and Control Meditation

Come to a comfortable position that allows your body to relax and rest.

Let your cheeks droop. Feel the tension in your jaw begin to dissipate.

Allow your eyelids to close, or if you're comfortable, keep them open.

Your meditation is your personal space.

As you open your heart to self-awareness today,

Picture yourself at the top of a mountain.

Here you are far away from your center –

High above the ground, anxious, and unaware.

But the comfort of solid ground is within your grasp.

With each number from ten to one, imagine yourself taking a step.

Closer, forwards, towards something better.

Ten.

Take a step. Feel your body accepting rest.

Nine.

Take a step. Feel your mind begin to slow.

Eight.

Take a step. With every number, you sink closer into deep awareness.

Seven.

Take a step and listen to your breath – your shallow gasps have changed to long, deep inhales. You're approaching your center.

Six.

The top of your journey is far behind you, and the tension you held has left.

Inhale for four counts – one, two, three, and four –

And exhale for four counts – one, two, three, four.

Take your last five steps, and with each one, give yourself over to complete surrendered awareness.

Five…four…three…two…one.

Here is your spiritual center. You are grounded, mentally, but you have not grounded your physical being.

Let us return to your awareness and return to your breath.

There is no fear of awareness – only acceptance and knowledge.

Feel the shallow inhale of your breath.

You have not found your breathing center.

Awareness will help you find it, and in turn, will bring you healing.

Take a deep breath in through your nose for one, two, three, four,

Extending your stomach outwards like a reach.

Breathe out now, through your mouth, one, two, three, four,

Collapsing your stomach against your spine.

You are a breathing being – breath is your life.

Focus your awareness. Focus your breathing. You are in control.

Calm any external thoughts – exhale them with your breath.

You are in the presence of your own spirit, and your breath brings it life.

Inhale for one, two, three, and four –

And exhale, for one, two, three, four.
As you inhale, search for knowledge.
One, two, three, four –
Survey your body while you exhale for one, two, three, and four.
 If there is tension, seek it out.
Where there is a pain, find it.
Inhale for one, two, three, and four –
And exhale for one, two, three, and four.
Focus your awareness upon that which isn't aligned with your center.
Inhale and feel the tension – one, two, three, four.
Exhale, and purge your system of impurities.
Keep your mind and thoughts centered upon your misalignment –
For three deep breaths, allow your mindful state to focus only here.
Breathe and purge.
Inhale your tension – one, two, three, and four –

And exhale unnecessary stress for one, two, three, and four.

Inhale for one, two, three, and four;

And exhale for one, two, three, and four.

Inhale for one, two, three, and four;

And exhale for one, two, three, and four.

Your awareness no longer belongs to this region –

You have focused, found, and freed.

Return, now, to your ten-step journey.

You begin your ascent cleansed and clean.

Step forwards, up. One.

Feel your strength. Reaching the peak is no longer difficult.

Two. Higher, stronger. You are aware. You are calm.

Three. Four. Take a breath.

Inhale for one, two, three, four,

And exhale for one, two, three, and four.

Step up. Five. Six. Seven.

Up, eight. Nine. Ten.

Inhale for one, two, three, four,

And exhale for one, two, three, and four.

You have returned, but you are not the same.

You are centered. You have control.

Open your eyes slowly – awareness is a gift.

Stress and Workplace Awareness Meditation

As you enter into your meditative practice today, settle in a comfortable position that won't require shifting.

With your palms open and relaxed wherever you feel most natural,

Allow your eyelids to droop if they feel heavy, or gently flutter open if you prefer.

Through your nose, inhale for four counts – one, two, three, four,

And exhale for four counts out your mouth – one, two, three, four.

Self-healing doesn't always involve the self; as you calm your thoughts,

Focus your mindfulness on stress – work, school, errands, and deadlines.
Focus your mindfulness on stress – work, school, errands, and deadlines.
Inhale for one, two, three, four,
And exhale for one, two, three, and four.
Your stress is an elevator on the top floor –
Suspended, heavy, damage-inflicting.
You begin high up, caught, and trapped.
Inhale for one, two, three, four,
And exhale for one, two, three, and four.
As your mindfulness stretches to wrap around your stress,
Feel the burden deep inside you.
To rid yourself of negativity, you must first root out its cause.
Where do you feel that your stress comes from?
Are you too busy at work? Anxious? Tired? Find your cause.
Find your root.
Inhale for one, two, three, four,

And exhale for one, two, three, and four.

Fixate on the cause of your imbalance – stress cannot come from where it doesn't belong.

Negative emotions have no place in your mental space.

Leave work at work – allow yourself the luxury of a safe place.

Inhale for one, two, three, four,

And exhale for one, two, three, and four.

Move your elevator down one floor. Heavy, difficult – but relief is close.

Feel your burden lighten – feel your spirits rise as tension falls.

You are closer to the floor, no longer dangerously on edge.

The cable above your head no longer strains with stress – but your mind remains tight.

Move gently down another floor, your mechanism creaking, shaking, but relaxing.

Your elevator cannot fall if you have brought it to the ground.

Inhale for one, two, three, four,
And exhale for one, two, three, and four.

Stress can spill over to become anxiety or anger – bring your elevator down, and allow this floor to purge your negative emotions.

Here, you are angry, hurt, embarrassed – overworked, tired, disillusioned.
You cannot stay. And you won't.

Leave behind these dangerous emotions – if they build too strongly, your elevator crashes.

Self-healing takes times, and self-healing takes strength.

Do not let your stress prove you weak.

Pull your elevator down again, inhaling for one, two, three four,

Exhaling negativity for one, two, three, and four.

Feel your breath, like your elevator, push the pain aside.

You cannot control what causes you stress, but you can help your mind bring your spirit back to the center.

There is no time for undue stress that we cannot ourselves change.

Pull down again, another floor. Each is softer, each is easier.

Your elevator plays your music – allow yourself to relax.

Inhale for one, two, three, four,

And exhale for one, two, three, and four.

With one final pull, bring your elevator down to the ground floor.

Inhale your safe solid state – one, two, three, four;

And exhale your doubt – one, two, three, four.

Steady your mind, and clear away any thoughts of work or stress.

You are centered here. Give no more of your time to stress.

Your minutes are yours, your thoughts are yours, and your elevator is yours.

Inhale for one, two, three, four,

And exhale for one, two, three, and four.

Here, your journey ends and begins. You are centered and grounded, spiritually and physically. Only you can allow your elevator to be drug back up.

Hold your ground – you are in control.
Inhale for one, two, three, four,
And exhale for one, two, three, and four.
Go mindfully into your stressful spaces with the center, control, and focus.

Slowly, open your eyes, and allow yourself to exist stress-free.

Abdominal Breathing

Abdominal breathing, unlike breathing meditation, focuses a bit more on your physical muscles than on your spiritual and emotional breathing as it relates to your inner peace. Abdominal breathing meditations are helpful in allowing your body to fill your bloodstream with oxygen – which creates, in turn, an incredible sense of calm, fulfillment, and bodily health. Most of us have no idea how to breathe properly using our diaphragm muscles, nose, and mouth – we simply do our best, without learning the proper technique to maximize our airflow and really enrich your body with oxygenated biological mindfulness. In order to properly meditate with abdominal breathing techniques, you're going to want to focus on breathing in through your nose, and out through your mouth. It might not sound very complicated, but the basic idea behind abdominal breathing meditations is to hone your breath to treat your body better. When you breathe in through your nose, to properly engage your diaphragm, you have to extend your stomach out and downwards, as if you are pressing the oxygen down into the lowest part of your belly. Once you've completed your inhale, you should collapse your stomach in an upwards motion while exhaling through your mouth. Instead of filling your belly to the very bottom, your exhale should be about starting from the bottom and pushing the oxygen out. Try this pattern a few times, and once you get the hang of it, you should start to feel your body tingle, relax, and fill with oxygen. When your bloodstream is highly oxygenated, your brain, heart, muscles, and organs function more effectively. Let's walk through a quick abdominal breathing meditation to teach you how to move your diaphragm, before getting into a full abdominal breathing mindfulness meditation script.

When you engage in abdominal breathing meditation, you'll want to make sure you are positioned so that your spine is straight and your upper abdomen isn't bent in a way that obstructs your airways. While most individuals choose to sit down in a comfortable cross-legged position on a soft matt or pillow, everyone is different – as long as your airways aren't being constricted, your abdominal breathing will function normally. Close your eyes, and let us begin.

Abdominal Breathing for Oxygenation

Relax. Feel your body enter into a mindful state.
Allow your heart to begin self-healing.
Your only focus now is breath.
In, and out.
In, and out.
Feel your heartbeat.
Inhale slowly through your nose,
Extending your stomach outwards for one, two, three.
Exhale slowly through your mouth, as you push
Your breath for three, two, one, up and out.
You collapse only to open – feel the cycle.

Inhale again, this time pushing your air
Down low into your belly.
Exhale slowly, pushing from that same deep
Up from the bottom –
Three, two, one.
Feel your diaphragm stretch, contract, and shift.
You are breathing as the universe intended.
Allow your bloodstream to fill with oxygen –
Your breath is your life.
Inhale through your nose, one, two, three, four,
Pushing your stomach out-outs,
Then exhale slowly, through your mouth,
One, two, three, four,
Pushing up – up, breathing with your diaphragm.
Center your focus on breathing only,
Your stomach, out, diaphragm, up,
Over and over, a nourishing pattern.

Inhale for one, two, three, four,
And exhale for one, two, three, and four.
Inhale for one, two, three, four,
And exhale for one, two, three, and four.
Inhale for one, two, three, four,
And exhale for one, two, three, and four.
Feel your muscles begin to remember how to use your diaphragm.
With every breath, in and out, your body remembers how to breathe.
Deep, long, slow – strong.
Breathe with your whole body.
Inhale for one, two, three, four,
And out for one, two, three, and four.
Learning and teaching take patience –
You are both student and teacher.
Your body is strong,
You are filled with oxygen – your breath is your life.
Allow your muscles to work freely;
A freely breathing body brings levity to the soul.
Inhale for one, two, three, four,

And exhale for one, two, three, and four.
Remember the way your muscles work –
Remember the way your breath feels.
Inhale for one, two, three, four,
And exhale for one, two, three, and four.
Work your stomach, feel your abdominals.
You are mindful and aware – your breath has never been stronger.
Inhale for one, two, three, four,
And exhale for one, two, three, and four.
Let your mind control your body –
Let your body heal your spirit.
Inhale for one, two, three, four, remembering your movements.
Exhale for one, two, three, and four – a repeating pattern.
Your breath is ancient, a combination of all your body, mind, and spirit –
But you are mindful, and a mindful heart can train their breath.
Inhale for one, two, three, four,
And exhale for one, two, three, four – you are growing as you breathe.

Slowly allow your pace to loosen.
Release control over your breath.
Feel how your muscles recreate the pattern.

You now know your ancient breath – remind your body how to use it.

Abdominal Breathing for Impulse Control

Inhale naturally for four counts – one, two, three, four,
And exhale naturally for four counts – one, two, three, four.
Center your mindfulness on only your breath:
Are your inhales shallowly? Are your exhales short?
Center your mindfulness on only your spirit –
Allow your breath to draw out your negativity.

Bring to mind your stressors, but don't allow them to affect your center.

Hold your pain in focus – and breathe, slowly.

Inhale for one, two, three, four,
But exhale sharp, quick, fast –

Loving and Kindness Meditation

Kindness Meditation for Self-Care

Practicing kindness towards oneself take time and patience.

Approach your meditation today with an open heart – not for the world, but for yourself.

As you come to rest in a comfortable prone position, allow your eyes to gently close against your cheeks.

Feel the breath enter and exit your body – inhale for one, two, three, four,

And exhale, for one, two, three, four.

You are three beings together – spirit, body, and mind, and you must nurture each with kindness.

As you feel yourself settle into a mindful state, imagine you are sinking through the floor.

You are not heavy with burden, or heavy with pain –

Your spirit, body, and mind, are heavy with calm, and in practicing self-kindness, you invite peace to join you.

Inhale for one, two, three, four, and exhale, for one, two, three, four.

The rise of your chest brings life to all you are – but all you are sometimes can suffer from the stress of life.

You are gentle – and must treat yourself so.

Take your spirit, body, and mind into your hands, and allow your meditation to reinvigorate your being with kindness.

Shift your focus onto your center. Imagine, in the middle of your chest, a glowing light.

This light is your love for your own self – created within, and nurtured within.

Inhale for one, two, three, four, and watch your light grow.

Exhale for one, two, three, and four.

Inside your chest, your light is larger – brighter – kinder.

While you focus on enlarging the light inside your chest, breath in for one, two, three, four, and out, for one, two, three, and four.

Keep your palms open to the universe as you feed your inner light.

Inhale for one, two, three, four, glowing from arm to arm.

Exhale for one, two, three, four, and feel the light reach down to your fingers.

You are a being lit in kindness, kindness created by you, for you.

Once more breathe in for one, two, three, four, igniting your body in the light as you exhale – one, two, three, and four.

Wreath yourself in kindness. You are your best lover.

Turn your mindful brain inwards towards your spirit.

Send light in waves to bathe your passions, dedication, motivation, and satisfaction.

You deserve to be kind to yourself.

Move from your spirit onto your body.

Allow your light to warm.

Inhale for one, two, three, four, and feel the sun against your skin.

Exhale one, two, three, and four – and let your fingers tingle.

All across your physical being, send waves of light and kind intentions.

Our physical beings are often overlooked, but you cannot be whole without all three selves.

Your physical being keeps you alive. Your physical being keeps you safe.

Treat your body with love. Treat your body with kindness.

Cruel words cannot change what you cannot change – kindness is acceptance, and acceptance is self-love.

Breathe in for one, two, three, four,

And out for one, two, three, and four.

Turn now to your mind, that dusty place with anxious thoughts and sharp fears.

Your mind is sacred, the home of your creativity, yourself, and your drive.

Bathe your mind in kindness – you are smart, you are strong, and you are capable of anything.

Inhale for one, two, three, four,

And exhale for one, two, three, and four.

Once more take stock of the weight of your body – you are heavy, thick, laden down with density;

But it is all love.

You are heavy with love.

Kindness is not easily found outside, but instead better cultivated inside your mind.

You can glow, on your own, and heal, on your own.

You are spirited, body, and mind – and if you are kind, you can do anything.

Inhale for one, two, three, four, and feel your glow begin to lighten.

You are a beacon of kindness – and your work, for now, is finished.

Inhale for one, two, three, four,

And exhale one, two, three, and four.

Absorb the light you left behind, taking in what wasn't used.

Slowly, dimly, bring yourself to a soft low burn.

Your kindness is a lamp inside your chest.

Find its glow when you need it most, but never let the light die out.

Inhale for one, two, three, four,

And exhale, kind, lit in light, for one, two, three, and four.

Gently allow your eyes to open. You re-enter the world as one –

Kindness forged, you are spirit, body, and mind at peace.

Love Meditation for Actualization

Settle into yourself.

Allow your physical being to disconnect from your spirit.

Here, and now, you are two separations – a vessel and a traveler.

Sink down into a comfortable position.

Allow your eyes to shut gently, or lightly rest open on a gentle face.

Inhale for four counts – one, two, three, four,

And exhale for four counts – one, two, three, four.

Your rhythm is your guide. Let your breath relax your body.

Focus your mindfulness upon your heart.

Listen to the steady beat, and feel the weight of your own humanity.

We all listen to the same beat – we all contain the same heart.

Inhale for one, two, three, four, and picture a vase filled with flowers –

But empty of water.

Inhale for one, two, three, four, and exhale, for one, two, three, four.

The empty space at the bottom of the vase calls to you –

But what can you do?

Inhale for one, two, three, four,

And exhale for one, two, three, and four.

You have something to pour.

Return your focus to your chest.

You have love there.

Love to give.

Every slow inhale of breath, the picture that vase with a thin pool of water.

Breathe in for one, two, three, four,

And out, for one, two, three, and four.

Each petal moves, there is water there.

You cannot receive love if you are incapable of giving.

Inhale for one, two, three, four,

And exhale for one, two, three, and four.

Each flower, thirst, feel your compassion – learn to give so that you may receive.

Learn to give so that you may receive.

Inhale for one, two, three, four, and give your love away.

Exhale one, two, three, and four – and watch the flowers in your vase.

As you breathe, you give, and you learn to love.

No closed heart can receive emotion.

Inhale for one, two, three, four,

And exhale for one, two, three, and four.

Make a promise to yourself, like each returning breath –

Love given is love returned.

Love given is love returned.

Love given is love returned.

Inhale for one, two, three, four,

And exhale for one, two, three, and four.

You are a vessel and a traveler, a being and a spirit.

But love is both physical and spiritual.

One brings the other, and the other brings one.

Spiritual love breads physical love, and physical love breads spiritual love.

You are a pattern, a circle, a cycle.

Your love comes from your heart – within – and returns, to heal you, also within.

Inhale for one, two, three, four,

And exhale for one, two, three, and four.

Body and spirit, mind and matter. Love is both.

Give yourself permission to give your love away –

Only once you've done so will love to return your way.

As you begin to slowly surface, inhale for one, two, three,

And exhale for one, two, and three.

Allow your palms to close, slowly.

Body and spirit, mind and matter. Love is both.

And you are love.

Self-Compassion "Break" Meditation

Forgiveness Guided Self-Healing

As you settle into your practice, find a comfortable position.

Give yourself permission to slow down.

Forgiveness does not come easy on our own hearts –

Extend yourself the same courtesy you do to others.

We are gentle to our surroundings and gentle to our families.

We love others, animals, and the planet – but we fail to love ourselves.

Let your eyes fall however they like; keep your palms open, no matter your stance.

Invite the universe into your heart. Leave your personal space open for positivity.

Slowly, inhale through your nose, for one, two, three, four.

Exhale, slowly, through your mouth, one, two, three, and four.

Focus your mindfulness as you breathe, for one, two, three, four,

Find the compassion your mindfulness inspires –

Compassion for yourself will heal old wounds.

A centered being cannot be at odds within itself.

A mindful life must mind itself.

Inhale slowly, for one, two, three, four,

And exhale, one, two, three, and four.

If you come to your practice with guilt today, find it and hold it in your mind.

If you come to your practice with anger today, find it and hold it in your mind.

If you come to your practice with insecurity today, find it and hold it in your mind.

We, like the world, have many sides, many faces, and many hides.

You are not defined by a single one – all are many, but in love, we are one.

Inhale through your nose for one, two, three, four,

And release through your mouth, one, two, three, and four.

A body divided cannot find its center.

You must unite yourself with love.

Begin by extending yourself compassion.

Then, extend yourself protection.

You are safe to forgive – and you are not your mistakes.

Inhale deeply through your nose, one, two, three, four,

Focusing on the pain that you are holding in your mind.

Exhale for one, two, three, and four –

Cruelty towards ourselves hurts twice as much as others.

You are not your greatest critic; do not harm that which keeps you alive.

Even when you err, your mind, body, and spirit are precious.
Growth is learning, growth is recovery;
And forgiveness fuels that growth.
Do not let guilt make your spirit heavy.
Do not let anger make your spirit spiteful.
Do not let insecurity diminish your light.
You are powerful and capable of change.
Breathe in through your nose for one, two, three, four,
And out through your mouth – not slowly this time. Fast, hard, all in one gust.
Aggressive, like the wind – a purification.
HUUUUUUUUHHHHHH.
Guilt, anger, insecurity, pain –
Blow them out, with each exhales.
Hard and fast, let your mouth make a sound.
Give yourself permission to expel negative energy.
Give yourself permission to make noise –
Push and push until your pain is gone.
Only peace will soon remain.

Inhale for one, two, three, and four –
And blow OUT – hard – all in one breath.
Let it all go.
Push it all out.
Your mistakes do no good trapped inside where they can hurt you.
Inhale for one, two, three, and four –
And blow – OUT. Your pain is the past.
Inhale, for one, two, three, and four –
And blow – OUT. Your pain is the past.
Inhale for one, two, three, and four –
And blow – OUT. Your pain is the past.
Forgive yourself.
Inhale your pain, breathe in your hurt.
Expel compassion – be kind to your heart.
Inhale for one, two, three, and four –
And be gentle to your exhale – one, two, three, four.
You are forgiven now. Your mind is clear, your body is purged.
Your blood runs compassion.
There is love for yourself here, and in love for yourself, there is healing.

Let go of your guilt. Let go of your anger. Let go of your insecurities.

You are forgiven. You are mindful and compassionate.

You are a centered being.

Inhale your hard work for one, two, three, four,

And exhale your peace – one, two, three, four.

Inhale your past – one, two, three, four,

And exhale your peace – one, two, three, four.

Inhale your pain – one, two, three, four,

And exhale self- love – one, two, three, four.

Let forgiveness return your soul to center.

Move forward – and treat yourself with care.

Universal Compassion Meditation

Vipassana Meditation

One of the most ancient forms of Buddhist meditation involving only the recognition of the sense, Vipassana meditation is the building block for modern emotional control. Vipassana meditation seeks to relax your mind and focus only on the rising and falling of your natural body processes (i.e., your natural breathing). However, when you practice Vipassana, you want to make special note of the sensations you experience while you practice. For this style of meditation for guided self-healing, you'll want to sit somewhere quiet, either in nature or near nature, in a comfortable enough position that you won't have to move for a long while.

Come to your natural breath with respect and admiration.

Breathing is part of your life force – do not force what is natural.

Allow yourself to recline, comfortable, safe, and steady.

With your palms open to the sky and universe, close your eyes.

Breathe in for four counts – one, two, three, four,

And out for four counts – one, two, three, four.

Clear your mind. You want to purge your thoughts, slow your mind.

It is time for quiet.

It is time now for only your senses.

You are in communion with your existence – nature, earth, body, breath.

One.

As you breathe, think only of that.

Breathing.

You are breathing.

Do not allow your thoughts to intrude upon this space.
Your mind should be clear, clean, and pure.
Only breathing.
You are only breathing.
If your mind begins to wonder,
You are only thinking.
If you find yourself focused on your physical being,
You are only Feeling.
You are a body filled with sensation –
But you are also a body overwhelmed by it.
Inhale for one, two, three, four,
And exhale for one, two, three, and four.
Do not allow your complicated existence to intrude upon your silence.
Here, you are alone with only your feelings.
They are all that matter.
Breathing.
You are only breathing.
Inhale for one, two, three, four,

And exhale for one, two, three, and four.
A sound might pass – but you cannot help Hearing.
Acknowledge the action – I am hearing.
But do not allow it to stay past its welcome.
You are not Hearing or Smelling, You are not thinking.
A scent may pass – but don't stall while you're Smelling.
You are not Smelling –
You are only breathing.
Note, and then erase.
Breathing.
Breathing.
You are only breathing.
Inhale for one, two, three, four,
And exhale for one, two, three, and four.
Your thoughts do not belong here –
Your feelings do not belong here –
Your smells do not belong here –
Your sounds do not belong here –
Here is only peace.

Here is the rest.
Here is quiet.
Here, you breathe.
In – one, two, three, four.
Out – one, two, three, four.
The simplest form of focus, here, in only your breath, upon only your life.
You need nothing but air.
You need nothing but breath.
Quiet your mind – You are only breathing.

Anxiety Meditation

Many individuals who struggle with anxiety or depression have individualized scripts and routines that help them manage their symptoms. However, there are a few general concepts and meditative techniques that can help almost anyone meditate for their anxiety. While these scripts might not be fool-proof for every form of anxiety or anxiety disorder, any sort of meditation or mindfulness is scientifically proven to help manage them. Let's get started.

General Self-Healing Script for On-The-Spot Anxiety Relief

Find a comfortable space where you feel most safe.

Center your mindful brain upon your breath.

Let your lungs fill with air – one, two, three, four.

Air brings your body life, and your breath keeps you safe.

Here and now, you are real. Focus only on what is real.

The present is now – and it safe for you here.

Exhale for one, two, three, and four.

Look around you. What do you see?

Name four things that you can find.

Inhale and count – one, two, three, four.

Each item, a breath. Feel your feelings de-escalate.

Exhale for one, two, three, and four.

Listen to your surroundings. What do you hear?

Name four sounds that you hear in your ears,

Breathe them in for one, two, three, and four.

And out, for one, two, three, and four.

Your surroundings help you ground your spirit. Hold yourself to the Earth.

You are present. Wherever you are where you can be. You can only control yourself.

Take charge of your breath – inhale for one, two, three, four, and hold –

Two, three, four - exhale, and feel your influence over your breath.

You are in control. Not your anxiety.

You are in control. Not your anxiety. You are grounded and ruled by your mindfulness.

Remind yourself.

Inhale for one, two, three, four – and relish in your ability to rest, here, where you have power.

No matter what happens around you,

Stress, tension, fear, pain – you, your mind, and your breath are safe.

These are yours. Find comfort in your body.

Find comfort in your center.

Breathe in for one, two, three, and four –
And out – one, two, three, and four.
Expel your fear. You have control.
Your center grounds you.
Your breath gives your life.
All you need is you.

Guided Anxiety Meditation for Active Brains

As you come to your practice today, keep a slow, steady pace –

You are here to calm, here to rest, and here to slow down.

Find a restful position with your palms gently open.

Inhale for four counts – one, two, three, four,

And out for four counts – one, two, three, four.

Focus on your chest, the rising and falling of your natural breath.

Your mind and anxiety pull you off center, further from stability.

But you are strong – you can pull them back.

Inhale for one, two, three, four,

And exhale for one, two, three, and four.

Focus on your brain now, your thoughts, your words, and your constant stream of sounds.

You are thinking, thinking, but you seek only quiet.

Return to your breath.

Inhale for one, two, three, four,

And exhale, for one, two, three, four.

As you breathe, focus your thoughts on a single chant.

One word, strong, powerful.

Mindful.

Clear.

Breathing.

Breathing.

Breathing.

Inhale for one, two, three, four,

And exhale for one, two, three, and four.
Allow your body to chant, consistent, focused – mindful.
Breathing.
You are breathing.
Feel your body revel in breath and silence.
If your mind begins to stray – bring it back to the center.
Breathing. Chant. You are breathing. Thinking comes later.
For now, only breathing.
Inhale for one, two, three, four,
And exhale for one, two, three, and four.
Let the rise and fall of your chest relax your muscles.
Your mind can rest – it is okay to rest.
Thinking becomes Worrying,
Breathing is living.
Inhale for one, two, three, four,
And exhale for one, two, three, and four.
Your mind is not in control while your breath rules your focus.

Your mind is not in control. Your breath rules your focus.

Breathing.

Breathing.

The activity has a place, but only with your permission.

Your mind is under your domain.

You have absolute control.

You are breathing.

There is no room for thinking.

Breathing.

Breathing.

Inhale for one, two, three, four,

And exhale for one, two, three, and four.

Inhale for one, two, three, four,

And exhale for one, two, three, and four.

Breathing.

You are breathing.

There is no room for anxious thoughts on a breath of air.

Let your mind calm. Every exhale, your mind quiets.

Inhale for one, two, three, four,

And exhale, silence – one, two, three, four.
Inhale – one, two, three, four,
And exhale, silence – one, two, three, four.
Breathing only.
Breathing only.
Inhale – one, two, three, four,
And exhale, silence – one, two, three, four.
Come to rest in silence.
Allow your peace to quiet.
You are calm. You are breathing.
Your mind is silent.
Your breath is strong.
Inhale –one, two, three, four,
And exhale one, two, three, and four.
You are calm. Your mind rests.

Finally, if you found this book useful in any way, a review is always appreciated!

www.ingramcontent.com/pod-product-compliance
Lightning Source LLC
Chambersburg PA
CBHW060410080526
44583CB00012B/523